Soulful Prayers VOL. 2

Soulful VOL. 2 Prayers

THE POWER OF INTENTIONAL COMMUNICATION WITH GOD

CHERYL POLOTE-WILLIAMSON

purposely created PUBLISHING

SOULFUL PRAYERS, VOL. 2

Published by Purposely Created Publishing Group™
Copyright © 2020 Cheryl Polote-Williamson
All rights reserved.

Scriptures marked NIV are taken from the New International Version®. Copyright © 1973, 1978, 1984, 2011 by Biblica, Inc.™. All rights reserved.

Scriptures marked NKJV are taken from the New King James Version®. Copyright © 1982 by Thomas Nelson. All rights reserved.

Printed in the United States of America

ISBN: 978-1-64484-173-0

This book is dedicated to the most faithful prayer warrior I know, my mother, Gretta Polote.

TABLE OF CONTENTS

FOREWORD

While it is true that we can pray anytime or anywhere, what I also love doing is going into one of our bedroom closets, so that I can spend proper quiet time with God. To begin, I close the door, make myself comfortable, read a short passage of Scripture from my Bible, and then I pray according to Matthew 6:9. Why? Because from the time I was old enough to learn words, as well as how to articulate them, my mom and maternal grandparents began teaching me how to recite The Lord's Prayer. I was a very small girl back then, but even today, I still recite that wonderful prayer daily. Then, when I am finished, I continue praying and honoring God with thanksgiving—I thank Him for allowing me to see another day . . . I thank Him for His unconditional love, mercy, and grace . . . I thank Him for all He's done, all He's doing, and all He's going to do in the future... I thank Him for absolutely everything. From there, my prayer becomes much more specific, and I begin asking Him to heal those who are ill—spiritually, mentally, emotionally, or physically—and to give strength, comfort, peace, and understanding to those who have lost loved ones. I pray for God's protection and safety for my husband, family members, friends, acquaintances, people I don't know personally, and myself. I also pray for anyone who has asked me to pray for them individually. I then pray for God's guidance, peace, and unity throughout the world.

I pray daily, multiple times, because prayer works.

It always has. More importantly, prayer is how I communicate with God in a direct, intentional, and serene manner. Through prayer, I am able to have an intimate conversation with our heavenly Father, our Lord and Savior Jesus Christ, and the Holy Spirit—up close and personal—candidly and consistently.

In *Soulful Prayers, Vol. 2: The Power of Intentional Communication with God*, Cheryl Polote-Williamson, along with her forty-four co-authors, has written the kinds of powerful prayers—inspiring, reflective, heartfelt prayers—that will totally reignite your entire prayer life. These amazing prayers will help sustain you in your darkest hours and lift you up during times of heartache, pain, and disappointment. They will encourage you to stay connected with God in the precious way He wants us to... every day of our lives.

Kimberla Lawson Roby
New York Times Bestselling Author
and Inspirational Speaker

Dr. Pasha Carter

FROM TEST TO TESTIMONY

Dear God,

I open my heart and drop to my knees humbly with thankfulness and servitude. Thank You for Your unconditional love, Your many blessings, and Your vision for me and my business. I ask, oh God, that You show me what's next for me in life. I have failed over and over again, Lord. But during each failure, I found the lesson that You were giving me, even when I didn't want to see it. I ask that You move me in the direction that You see fit for me; though I may not understand it, my faith is in You, Lord.

Sharpen my skills, and use me to bless and uplift others, Lord. For every door that You open for me, allow me to open twice as many for others. Lord, when I am tired and weary, give me strength. When I am out of ideas and strategies, fill me with Your infinite wisdom.

Lord, You have brought me through many tests that I thought I would fail and allowed the tests to be a testimony.

Lord, I want to be Your vessel. Lord, allow Your light to shine on me and Your words and wisdom to flow through me to touch the souls of those that may be where I have been in business and life. Allow me to forgive those who have wronged me in business that I may open my heart to new ventures and collaborations. Lord, I am asking You to help guide me as I lead the way and allow me to be an example of true servant leadership.

Amen.

Reflective Scripture:
Luke 12:31

Tiffany Easley

CONQUERING PHYSICAL ILLNESS

Dear God,

I thank You that my physical (natural) body is in alignment with Your supernatural design and intent. My body is whole, there is nothing missing, lacking, or broken. I declare and decree that all diseases, infirmities, and ailments will no longer reside in my body. I speak to every chronic and terminal illness that has been assigned to invade or attach itself to my cardiovascular; digestive; endocrine; immune; integumentary; lymphatic; muscular; nervous; reproductive; respiratory; skeletal; and urinary systems, cancelling its assignment; stripping its authority; and nullifying its power.

God, my body is Your temple and I will make wise choices concerning my health. I will monitor what I ingest, digest, and consume. I will treat my body as the temple You created it to be and will preserve it by getting annual health screenings and exams. I will pay attention to my body when the need for adequate mental, physical, and emotional rest arises.

From this day forward, I declare and decree a life of health and wholeness. I take authority over my health, and I speak total healing and restoration into the atmosphere with faith and expectation . . . health and healing belong to me. I am healthy and whole NOW!

I speak my healing into the atmosphere and affirm it by boldly declaring these words in Your presence . . .

I AM committed to my health and my healing.

I MAKE wise choices concerning my health and healing.

I SPEAK good health and healing into the atmosphere for myself, my family, and everyone divinely connected to me.

Healing, healthiness, and wholeness ARE mine!

In Jesus' name!

Amen.

Reflective Scripture:
3 John 1:2

Russell M. Williamson Sr.

LIFE IS FILLED WITH SWIFT TRANSITIONS

Dear God,

You are the master of all things and Your sovereignty is undeniable. For that reason, I kneel right now humbling myself before You, Lord. I praise Your name right now, Lord, because everything I have experienced and everything I have been through is because of Your divine guidance in my life. Heavenly Father, I know You are directing or allowing all of these things to happen for the shaping and sharpening of my spirit. I pray Your Word for it says You know the plans You have for me. Lord, You plan to prosper me and to give me hope and a future.

Lord, I know You will strengthen me during this period of transition. Help me to embrace the uncertainty and realize that my faith is in You, not in man. You have commanded me to be strong and courageous because You are with me. You, Father, have gone ahead of me because when one door has closed You have been sure to open another one. However, Father God, give me patience while I wait in the hallway.

Heavenly Father, life is filled with so many swift changes. Sometimes I can see them coming and other times they seem to come from nowhere. Lord, let me not lean on my own understanding. Let me be of the mind to acknowledge You and submit to Your guidance. Give me strength, knowledge, and wisdom to follow the path the Holy Spirit prompts me to follow. Your way, Jesus, is definitely the straight way to Your blessings.

Lord Almighty, I accept that You are doing a new thing and it will spring up. Let me be faithful because You are always faithful. I declare that You will make a way and where others might perceive a wasteland, You will bring life and prosperity. Jesus, You are the same yesterday, today, and tomorrow. It is in the matchless name of Jesus Christ that I pray.

Amen.

Reflective Scripture:
Joshua 1:9

DON'T GIVE UP ON GOD BECAUSE GOD WON'T GIVE UP ON YOU!

Dear God,

You are the Most High God, the Almighty God, the Lord God Jehovah. Nothing is impossible for You. I thank You for Jesus, I thank You for the Holy Spirit, and I thank You for Your Word.

You said that I should bring everything to You in prayer. I have been diagnosed with glaucoma. I've had 10 procedures performed on my right eye. After the surgery, the surgeon stated that she wasn't sure if the surgery helped and we would have to wait to see what Mother Nature would do. My heart was heavy. I sat and cried for a while. Then, I remembered what You said in Your Word.

Your Word says sickness and disease is not of You. I am covered by the blood of Jesus and by His stripes I am healed. Father God, because I have received Your Son, Jesus, as my Lord and Savior, I am Your righteousness. Therefore, sickness and disease must respond to my body just as it responds to You. Since it cannot live in You, it cannot live in me because my body is the temple of the living God.

Lord God, I trust You with my whole heart and I will not lean to my own understanding, but in all my ways I acknowledge You. I know that I can speak to life's challenges and tell them to be gone and they move. I speak healing to my body because I have what I say. Manifest it, Father. Do it, God. I know You can do it! I won't give up on You, God, because I know You won't give up on me. In the precious and holy name of Jesus.

Amen.

Reflective Scripture:
Mark 11:22-24

STRONG AND COURAGEOUS AT-RISK SERVANT IN HIS PRESENCE

Dear God,

Thank You for Your presence during the times that I needed You as a military servant. Your presence while serving on hostile and friendly grounds was a blessing beyond measure when faced with the known and the unknown. Lord, I pray that I continue to do Your will gracefully and with gratitude. I vow to be Your courageous servant whose desire is to work wholeheartedly for the protection, defense, and well-being of others, even though such jobs seem to be tough and are often unappreciated. Lord, I pray that You allow me to remember that You will be with me wherever I go and in whatever I may go through. I thank You, Lord, for the reminder of Your sacrifices for the world then allowing me to undergo sacrifices while being one of Your strong and courageous servants to the world, my country, and my community. I pray that this prayer touches hearts with thoughts of gratitude whenever it encounters another strong and courageous servant of Yours. Lord, I pray that You provide me and other at-risk servants continued blessings and anointed strength so that You will be pleased with our efforts with the well-being of others as we continue to be Your servants.

Lord, every day as an at-risk servant, I have to make tough and complex choices. Assist me, Lord, to make sound decisions in every circumstance. Expose clarity to me, my Lord, and allow me to stay still and composed during tense moments when I encounter distressing situations. Allow me to cry out to You, Lord, whenever an unknown or undesired circumstance comes about, and I feel that dark second of uncertainty. Lord, I pray to always keep my eyes fixed upon You so that I can see what You see, Lord, knowing that You are with me wherever I go.

Amen.

Reflective Scripture:
Joshua 1:9

Dr. Onika L. Shirley

PRAYER FOR PERSEVERANCE WHILE BEING PERSECUTED IN THE WORKPLACE

Dear God,

Thank You in advance for keeping my brothers and sisters feet grounded when individuals in position try to uproot them from the very place You strategically planted Your sons and daughters. Thank You, Father, for sitting high above all else and looking into every plot of destruction. God, You know all things, and the negative things that are being said and done behind closed doors are being bound on Earth as it is in Heaven. God, thank You for sitting high and looking low, and watching over Your children during their times of distress. Thank You, Lord, for strength during the times of trouble in the workplace. Lord, thank You for giving us the tenacity and the audacity to press towards the mark when our enemies try to destroy us. God, I know You're right there while we wrestle with complicated circumstances in the workplace. Thank You, God, for not abandoning or forgetting about us when plots are being made. As we wait for You to intercede on our behalf, we praise You for all that You have already done and for what You are preparing to do. Lord, thank You for perseverance during our trials. Thank You, Lord, for the strength to withstand the test.

God, I thank You because You are my provider. God, I thank You because You said I am the head and not the tail. God, I thank You because You said You will never leave me nor forsake me. God, I thank You because You are my peace. God, You said no weapon formed against me shall prosper. God, thank You for uncovering the schemes of my enemies. God, thank You for Your truth. God, I know Your truth is living, active, powerful, and life changing. Thank You, Lord, for victory in my workplace trial.

Amen.

Reflective Scripture:
James 1:12

Katrice Gray

FOR ALL THE WAYS YOU'VE BLESSED ME, THANK YOU

Dear God,

This prayer is not to ask You for anything, but to thank You for the things that I can now recognize and appreciate as Your mighty hand in my life.

God, I thank You for keeping me stable when this world tries to eat me alive. I feel the strength of Your Love straightening my back as I hear You whisper to me that nothing shall overtake me on Your watch. I thank You for protecting my son as he navigates the path You have set for him. Thank You for keeping a hedge of protection around him and for trusting me with Your best. Thank You for keeping my home when I'm there and when I'm away.

Thank You for keeping me and the cars around me safe on the road when I am traveling these highways and byways.

God, I thank You for the pitfalls You saved me from because I was too stubborn to heed the warnings, and I appreciate the blessings You didn't allow to miss me although I was undeserving.

God, I thank You for making what I have more than enough. More than enough money to cover my bills, more than enough food to feed my family, more than enough sense to bless and praise You, more than enough compassion to serve in Your name, and an overflow to always be able to share knowing that I serve The Living Well that never runs dry.

God, continue to bless me, my family, my friends, my co-workers, and my frenemies.

Keep a calm tongue in my mouth and a sweet spirit about me. I could never love You enough, but daily and continually will I serve YOU.

Amen.

Reflective Scripture:
Isaiah 45:2

Dr. Peggie Etheredge Johnson

A PRAYER FOR LEADERS AND SPOUSES IN MINISTRY, MARKETPLACE, AND MISSIONS

Dear God,

I am thankful that You have called and chosen leaders along with their spouses to the important undertaking of leadership in ministry, the marketplace, and missions. I am especially thankful to You for spiritual leaders, governmental and civil leaders, and their spouses. You have chosen them and placed them in positions of power, authority, and personal sacrifice to be overseers and shepherds, sharing in the progress, protection, and preparation of Your people; for You have said that all souls belong to You, even the one that sins.

Father, I pray that all who lead know You personally in the power of Your mighty love through salvation in Jesus Christ and proclaim Him as their Savior. I ask that You endow them with the joy of loving what and who You love as they diligently do what is good, showing justice to everyone, and walking humbly with You.

Lord, furnish them with Your wisdom, knowledge, and understanding of You and Your Word as they walk upright before You. Please give them what they need to survive and thrive as they lead for Your purpose, Your glory, and Your will! Deliver them from every form of fear—self-fear, fear of others, and fear of Satan. Instead, equip them with a healthy and reverent fear of You.

Father, I pray that You lead them before they lead others and teach them before they teach others, as they freely submit themselves to Your authority in everything. I pray that You keep them spiritually, physically, and emotionally healthy to be enthusiastic and resilient. Surround them with authentic intercessors. Protect them from enemy friends, ministry mistresses and manstresses, and fabricated indictments. Father, reinforce their assignment, maintain their courage, preserve their marriages, and protect their children, in Jesus' name.

Amen.

Reflective Scripture:
Micah 6:6-8

Tiffany Mayfield

A BUSINESS OWNER'S PRAYER FOR SUCCESS AND GROWTH

Dear God,

I bow down before You grateful and thankful for Your protection over my family and my life. Thank You for this day. Thank You for calling me higher in good health and a clear mind. Father, I must thank You in advance for substantial success and growth in my business, including multiple locations and six and seven-figure increases of my finances. I thank You for calling my children and their friends and families higher, and for blessing their businesses, jobs, and finances, in Jesus' name. I declare that I will move forward from barely making it to being so blessed that I have more than enough. Lord, I declare that supernatural doors will open for me and every birthed vision with my name on it comes my way.

I count it all joy that You are working in my life, exalting my name in rooms where You have opened doors of opportunity. I thank You for calling me higher for Your glory. I thank You for bringing me up out of the trenches of laying low and playing small, for the Bible says greater are You that lives in me. Hallelujah! Lord, I thank You in advance for freeing us from the strongholds that held us hostage in our own minds. Father, I thank You that there is nothing too hard for You. I thank You that we will experience love, joy, and peace in the sweet name of Jesus. I declare by faith that no matter when weapons form, they will not prosper.

I love You, God. I commit my life, fresh and new, to You. I release my faith and I believe that my faith is before You now. I thank You that I am blessed, and generations are blessed in Your holy name. In the mighty name of Jesus.

Amen.

Reflective Scripture:
Psalm 46:1-3

Aliya Allen

ETIQUETTE—YOUR PRESENCE IS IMPORTANT

Dear God,

Thank You for blessing me with an understanding of the true definition of etiquette. Growing up, my mother made sure I was always surrounded by strong women and men who not only taught me how to respect myself, but others. I wasn't aware of the importance of business, dining, or social etiquette until opportunity brought me to corporate America to see the difference. The various positions in which I've served within the realm of business, professional women's organizations, and church have taught me that there is a manner in which you must conduct yourself. Lord, as I continue pursuing my passion for training youth and young adults in etiquette, I want them to also learn the importance of protocol and relationships. In all the decisions that we make in this life, we must seek an understanding of doing things right and we must know that there are ramifications when things are not done in decency and in order. Through trial and error, I realize that it is by Your grace, Father, that I have been blessed with a gift for teaching others how to conduct their business with dignity and excellence. As I learn more about etiquette through the model demonstrated by Your life and Your personhood, I ask that You reveal to me wisdom others can utilize to acquire success as meeting conductors, interview prospects, and table setters.

Lord, I know You want Your people to understand that etiquette is an extension of Your grace and Your justice. Please continue to place me in positions where I have the opportunity to show my neighbors that their presence is important.

Amen.

Reflective Scripture:
Ephesians 4:29

Dr. Eric L. Holmes

TRANSITION, TRANSFORMATION, AND TRANSPARENCY

Dear God,

I humbly come to You before the throne of grace. First, to say thank You for allowing me to endure the transition, to see the results of the transformation, and to be able to be transparent to help others.

Lord, through these stages, I have truly come to know You in a more intense way. I thank You and I love You, Lord, because my relationship with You is stronger than it's ever been. You have caused me to endure many trials and tribulations, but my end result has yielded victory. Father, You have given me the gift called victory.

You have created me to be a conduit of overcoming and transparency so that I may help many others realize the victory in their own lives. You have chosen me to be a vessel because You've allowed me to endure many different areas in my life which consisted of the three T's: transition, transformation, and transparency.

You have transitioned me to see a greater transformation into who You have ordained me to be. So, Father God, I love You and I owe You everything. I thank You for allowing me to cast all of my burdens and cares upon You because You care for me. In Jesus' name I pray.

Amen.

Reflective Scripture:
1 Corinthians 15:57

Juanita Payne

IN RECOURSE OF HOPE

Dear God,

I give You all the honor, all the glory, and all the praise. Lord, thank You for being our refuge and strength, and an ever-present help in the time of need. Father God, I thank You for the hope that You have given me when prayer was needed. I thank You for this mighty weapon of warfare that You have given us to fight against the enemy. Father, I thank You for allowing me to turn towards You first, oh God. I thank You for never leaving me or forsaking me, Lord God.

Father, You said to train up a child in the way he should go: and when he is old, he will not depart from it. Lord God, thank You for Your promise in Isaiah 43:2 that says, "When you pass through the waters, I will be with you; And through the rivers, they will not overflow you. When you walk through the fire, you will not be scorched, Nor will the flame burn you." I thank You for allowing my child to come back to a place of safety when the enemy was raging war against his mind, body, soul, and spirit. Thank You for bringing him back to a house of prayer.

Lord God, You said that faith is the substance of things hoped for, the evidence of things not seen. Therefore, Lord God, my faith is in You, no matter what it looks like. Thank

You for protecting my child and cancelling the plans the enemy had against him, Lord God. What the enemy meant for evil, You turned it around for his good. Father God, give him wisdom to know the schemes of the enemy so he will never fall prey again. In Jesus' name!
Amen.

Reflective Scripture:
Joshua 1:9

Marsha Taylor

LIVING FROM A PLACE OF EXPERIENCE

Dear God,

God of the universe.
> Teacher of my life.
> Master of my circumstances and healer of my mind.
> Maker of the impossible, sustainer of it all.
> The faithful God, my Father.
> Creator of us all, Abba Father is Your name.
> Abba Father, I come boldly before Your mercy seat as You are my compassionate God.
> Thank You for creating this new day and I'm glad that I am a part.
> Purge my inner thoughts and the deep recesses of my heart, where Your love is ever flowing in every new magnificent thought.
> Today, I speak life to my body, soul, and mind. And Lord, I never meant to worry because I am an heir of the kingdom of God!
> Abba Father, You created me in Your image and Your likeness.
> How can I NOT give You thanks from this place, as I constantly fall?

Lord, I recognize that Your decision to make me was not a mistake, it was always in Your thoughts.

You told me in Genesis, YOU are the creator and I am a part.

You orchestrated my existence, with a delightful heart.

I will never take You for granted Lord, because You are my superstar!

I recognize my scars should replicate the person that You are!

Today, I will sing a song of victory and dance among the stars.

Lord, my past is now history and I am committed to live from a place of experience with You.

Yes, Lord, I have come to know the reason for my existence, and I am excited to walk in it.

Please, Abba, help me to keep the distractions away and focus on my created path.

Today, I choose to reconnect, recommit, and receive my brand new start and become one with You in spirit as I continue to be transformed.

Lord and Father of the universe, the only true and wise God,

I thank You for this newfound confidence that's deep down in my heart.

You will forever be my refuge, my life, my eternal God.

I love You beyond measure.

You are the MASTER of it all.

Amen.

Reflective Scripture:
Romans 12:2

Tammy L. Woodard

LORD, PROTECT OUR SONS LIKE MOSES

Dear God,

Thank You for giving me the wisdom and knowledge to seek You in all things. Thank You for being my resting place when the pressures of life try to break me down. Thank for being a bridge over troubled waters. Father God, You said in Your Word, "Be still and know that I am God." So, Father, I am standing still and depending on You.

God, I need You right now. I am petitioning You on behalf of my sons and all sons of the world. Hide them from the snare of the enemy, just like You covered Moses from Pharaoh's soldiers. Lord, they need You like never before. Put a hedge of protection around them. Touch their hearts and minds so that they may seek Your face. Order their steps and uncover their eyes so that they will recognize the tricks of the enemy. Open their ears so they can hear Your voice and block out the distractions of the devil. Give them wisdom, guidance, and the will to serve You. Lord, whatever it is that they are seeking in this sinful world, I pray that they will find it in You. Heal the hurt and pain caused by others. Put the right people in their path that will point them to You. Lord, provide them with godly friends and a godly helpmate. Remove generational curses and toxic relation-ships. Remove the spirit of depression, entitlement, lying, theft, envy, bitterness, anger, pride, and addiction. Lord, I plead the blood of Jesus over their lives and demand all demonic spirits to leave and go back to the pit of hell. I thank You in advance, Father, for granting my request. I decree and declare that they are freed from the enemy's hand. In Jesus' name I pray.

Amen.

Reflective Scripture:
Psalm 138:7

A PRAYER FOR THE POWER TO FORGIVE

Dear God,

I have learned that I can't pray for my offender with sincerity until I first talk to You about my feelings from the offense. So, I begin by admitting that I am hurt, very hurt. I believe I don't deserve what was done against me because I did my best and meant no harm to anyone. Now, every time I see that person, I think about what happened. I try to let go of the pain, but it's hard. The unforgiveness has stolen my peace. But I know I won't heal until I forgive.

So, I ask You to heal my hurting heart. Help me to let go of this nagging ill will toward the person who hurt me. I want to forgive like You. Every time I ask for Your forgiveness, You give it to me without hesitation. I pray peace be restored between the person who hurt me and myself. I do not want us to be enemies, for Your Word tells me to live peaceably with people.

And, Father, when I fail or even sin, I pray that You give me the strength to forgive myself. Your will is that I stop beating myself up over past mistakes and sins, especially when Your Word says these things will work toward my good. Amen.

Reflective Scripture:
Colossians 3:13

Dr. John Dandridge

PRAYER FOR VETERANS FROM A WARRIOR

Dear God,

Thank You for Your divine protection of my parents, my siblings, and my entire family during my childhood years and my years of military service. Yet, even amid Your will, having a family that loves Jesus, and realizing all the joys of serving, military life is HARD! The military hurts and costs. It cost all of us something. I wear the scars to prove it. Deployments left me wondering if I would survive. I did. I come now just as I am—feeble, fragile, brokenhearted, and debilitated—to pray for past, present, and future Veterans, victims, families, and friends. God, console them during this moment of reflection.

I lift up every wounded warrior, disabled Veteran (DAV), prisoner of war (POW), and those missing in action (MIA) or killed in action (KIA), and countless families and friends throughout my 20 plus years of military service. Give me help, God, for each cause: PTSD, suicidal ideation, lost limbs, and moral injuries. Lord, 22 Veterans commit suicide daily during times of peace and war. My first real encounter with death, grief, and loss was the passing of my mother then my father (a Korean/Vietnam Veteran of more than 25 years) who are interred in Arlington National Cemetery. Our son was injured in Afghanistan and is now an amputee. I find myself feeling deep loss as each day passes. There's an emptiness in me that can't be filled unless You do it God. So, please help me make sense of this suffering I experience daily. I am humbled and grateful for survivors, family caretakers, and professionals who walk the road of a new normal with me!

Help us, O God, to keep the faith, and to keep loving and caring for those who have and are recovering.

I pray with adoration, confession, thanksgiving, and supplication in God's name.

Amen.

Reflective Scripture:
Ephesians 6:10-17

Marlo Mozee

GRACED IN
THE WILL OF GOD

Dear God,

Thank You for Your amazing grace of touching me with Your finger of love today. In this journey of life, I am deeply grateful for Your touch. As Your Word encourages and counsels me, I choose to be a light in the darkness. I pray to daily penetrate the darkness as Your light so that I may become a container of Your glory. Lord, I thank You for Your word of empowerment. You have graced me to carry out the clarion call of Your will. You have become ever-present in my spirit through Your incredible presence of peace, love, and joy as the fruits of Your Spirit soar. Teach me, oh Lord, Your mighty ways that I might become pleasing in Your sight.

Your ways and thoughts are higher than the Heaven and Earth, oh Lord. I declare Your mighty works through me. I pray that You continue to lead and guide me through the mountains, hills, valleys, and unexpected turns. Higher in You, Lord, is where I desire to be. Resting in You is what makes me know how complete I can be. Forever grateful I stand in You.

You've carefully placed me in this world to be a beacon: a light for the lost. I pray, oh Lord, that You continue to grace me. Grace me to lead in love. Grace me to follow Your path. And in Your grace, I will stand.

Amen.

Reflective Scripture:
2 Corinthians 12:9

Symonia A. Montgomery

STANDING IN EXPECTATION

Dear God,

I come to You as humbly as I know how, standing before You emotionally naked. I have endured things that have left me broken in my spirit. I fight to understand why I bore the burdens of sexual assault, physical and emotional abuse, even abandonment. I've carried these things with me daily and allowed them to weigh me down to the point of trying to take a life that wasn't mine to take. Yet, You thought I was worth saving. You snatched me back from the gates of hell and restored me, Your child, in ways only You could. You revealed that every situation was fitting into the plan YOU have for my life. You provided me with the ability to speak life into the lives of others amid their darkest hours. This assignment is not always easy because sometimes the enemy creeps in trying to convince me I'm worthless. So, right here and right now, I want to thank You for the strength to endure the path You have set before me. I may not always understand that path or even willingly accept it due to the pain so deeply intertwined within it, but I know that Your Word cannot return void. So, as the trials and tribulations of this life descend upon me, I ask that You increase my faith in You and Your Word. Remind me that ALL things are working together for my good. Permit me to stand in expectation of the blessings that lay before me. Lord, I beg of You not to tolerate anything less of me than what You have ordained for me. I know I am created in Your image. I am built to prevail. Therefore, no matter what comes, I will stand in expectation of greatness while trusting You and Your will for my life.

Amen.

Reflective Scripture:
Romans 8:28

WALKING IN PURE FORGIVENESS WITH GOD

Dear God,

Thank You, Father in Heaven, for creating in me a clean heart and a renewed spirit of forgiveness. You removed all anger, doubts, and resentment from my heart and mind and gave me the peace that surpassed all understanding.

Lord God, when I was experiencing anger and hurt, You spoke to me in a subtle voice and guided me to be still. My prayers during that difficult time were weak and I could not hear You. My life was filled with distractions, interruptions, and frustrations. I was anxious and confused to the place of feeling spiritually poor. Thank You for calming my spirit and allowing me to surrender my cares and give the control to You. I stopped trying to figure it all out and began trusting You with all my heart and soul. God, I heard You speak to me in quiet tones. I made a conscious decision to commit myself to listen to You and to trust You. After turning my will and ways over to You, I began feeling peace and happiness in a pure and perfect way. I discerned how to listen to Your voice during daily times of distractions, interruptions, and frustrations. Thank You, God, for showing me how to forgive in the purest way—in words and in actions. Father God, because of

You I am now living a stronger, wiser, and better life. Thank You for guiding me to forgive daily as I submit to Your will and way. You are an awesome God and I trust You.

Amen.

Reflective Scripture:
Matthew 6:14

Jessica L. Howard

FROM GROWING PAINS TO D.I.V.A.: LIFE IN FULL BLOOM

Dear God,

Hear my cry! Please heal this abandonment, pain, anxiety, and depression. Take away the shame of unworthiness. You chose to love and nurture me in spite of me. Teach me to serve You when it is hard. Help me to forgive those who judged me, rejected me, and hurt me.

Lord, how can someone full of love and compassion experience great suffering? I was raised by my maternal grandparents, and for most of my life I felt a void. I did not understand what I know now. You, heavenly Father, knew me before I was formed in the womb; You consecrated me! Jeremiah 1:5.

Weary from the disappointment, the little girl in me slowly died in the fight for understanding and acceptance. I asked You to release the pain, heal my broken heart, and help me to find my purpose. I could not move forward holding on to what was. You caused me to bloom after submitting to Your will. You saved me.

God, I know you have a purpose for me. Plans to prosper me and to give me a future. I don't know what it will look like, but I pray that it will be better than the days I've seen. Lord, help me to have strong faith and allow me the ability to Diligently and Intentionally Visualize Abundance in the plans You have for my life.

Thank You, Lord, for giving me life and for being my family! My grandmother who raised me died a year after I was baptized. In that season, I understood Your grace. It took a village to raise a child of God. I am blessed and grateful for the abundance of Your love.

Amen.

Reflective Scripture:
Psalm 68:5

FROM THE DEPTHS OF ME

Dear God,

I humbly come before You, asking that You protect and keep this marriage. I truly believe that You are able to mend the broken pieces and heal our hearts from any turmoil, hurt, pain, and grief. Help us to become selfless and to submit unto one another. Give us the courage to forgive and apologize when we have offended one other. Oftentimes, we find fault in our mate, but help us to see when we are in the wrong and take ownership. Thank You, Lord, for the development of true friendship, commitment, love, and respect for one another. Continue to bless this marriage and give us restoration, joy, grace, and peace. Remove strife, bitterness, pride, unforgiveness, resentment, or anything else that is harmful to this marriage. Help us not to be antagonistic or controlling. I pray that we will continue to be led by You and that we respect Your Word. Help us to listen and have effective communication. Show my spouse how to be loving, gentle, and considerate. Teach me how to love, honor, and respect my spouse. Help us to be wise in our speech and demonstrate kindness towards one another. Remove any fear, doubt, or worry that may try to creep into our hearts. I pray that You meet every emotional, financial, physical, and relational need in this marriage. Help us to serve one another in humility and strive to be intentional in meeting each other's emotional and physical needs. Remove any idle words that have been spoken and create a union of reconciliation. I thank You in advance for answering my prayer and hearing my heart's cry.

Amen.

Reflective Scripture:
Matthew 19:6

Sonya M. Hall-Brown

DELAYED BUT NOT DENIED

Dear God,

I now understand that Your delays are not denials. But, why do I feel as though I'm still in the wilderness when I know You have delivered me? Why do I need to forgive when I already understand that forgiveness brings great benefits in my health, my spirit, and my relationship with You? Even though I understand that forgiveness brings great benefits in my health, my spirit, and relationship with You, I know there will still be moments when I need to seek forgiveness for myself and others. God, You said I was fearfully and wonderfully made, and I thank You for reminding me that I can always refer to Psalm 139:14 in Your Word which reminds me of that. God, I applaud You for putting an anointing on everything that I've been through so that I can minister to young women and men with similar challenges. I am a survivor of the unfairness of this life. I'm a new creation in Christ! I'm about my Father's business. I choose to live! I choose to love because You are my heavenly Father, my first love who first loved me. You have never left or forsaken me. You have always been right by my side. Your promises for me were delayed yet never denied because of my unforgiveness! You never denied my blessings. I followed Your instructions and You restored me. You restored my broken marriage. You blessed me with my own business, which I use as a ministry tool. You have blessed our children beyond measure, and they have all confessed salvation. God, I have surrendered ALL! I lift my hands toward Heaven and thank You for all that You have done in my life and in the lives of our children, our grandchildren, and our great-grandchildren to come. Thank You for keeping us in the hollow of Your hand as we continue to reverence You as our Lord and our King!

Amen.

Reflective Scripture:
1 Peter 5:7

I MATTER! CREATED ON PURPOSE TO MAKE A DIFFERENCE

Dear God,

Father, I come to You wholly and humbly. The Bible said to love my neighbor as myself; therefore, I pray that you, Daddy God, teach me how to love me as you see me. Father, I pray that I become so in love and connected to You that when people see me they only see the love that You have given to me that overflows to them. I thank You for choosing me to represent You. Thank You for teaching me that I matter. I pray that I represent You well. God, I pray that Your Holy Spirit teaches me to stay focused on the call You created me for so that I owe no man nothing but Your love. Father, I pray that I have a heart after Your own heartbeat, and that I love what You love and do everything out of the love You have given me through Your Son, Jesus. Father, I pray that I only speak the words You give me. I pray that I speak with purpose and that I do what You have purposed me to do, unapologetically. I pray that my ears are tuned to Your frequency so that I may continue to hear Your voice and Your voice alone and go where You send me. I pray that as You love me, I love myself and that love flows unto the people You call me to. God, I pray that my feet stand fast to Your Word, that I study to show myself approved, and that it is bound in my heart. I pray that I am always prepared and willing to go where You send me while believing and trusting that You are in full control.

Amen.

Reflective Scripture:
Matthew 22:37-40

Jennifer Harris Nyanfor

A PRAYER FOR INNOVATION AND CREATIVITY FOR BUSINESS GROWTH

Dear God,

Your name is so marvelous in all the earth. Thank You for being an *innovative and creative* God. You are the creator of all things. From nothing You created the earth and with Your majestic voice, You declared Your vision into existence. You made man in Your image; therefore, we have Your attributes. You looked at everything You made, and it was very good.

I humbly bow myself before You, most high God, in adoration. I appeal to You, God, to give me the power to accomplish what You had in mind when You created me. I thank You for the business You have entrusted in my care. I pray to be a good steward and multiply the talents You have given me. Open doors for me, God, to surround myself with greatness and with those who will add value to my life. I ask that You give me Your divine inspiration and instructions on how to incorporate *innovation and creativity* into my business, for I know it is the roadmap to something incredible happening in my life. Release the creativity in my mind to conceive new ideas. Unleash the artistic and humanistic talents that have been dormant in my brain. Father, help me to abort those mediocre thoughts that have the potential to stump the growth of my business. Rejuvenate and cultivate my cognitive skills that I may think and perform on a level that will generate millions of dollars for my business.

I decree and declare that with Your help, God, I will use *innovation and creativity* in my business for Your glory and step out of my comfort zone to do something that has never been done before. I will be the ONE to start something extraordinary! In Jesus' name.

Amen.

Reflective Scripture:
Genesis 1:1-2, 27

RESTORE OUR RELATIONSHIP

Dear God,

You are omnipotent, omnipresent, and omniscient. You are the all-wise and merciful God. I love You and bless Your holy and divine name. I come to You, in Jesus' name, interceding on behalf of relationships. The examples around me functioned with a zeal of godliness and lacked foundational truth. I repeated the same generational cycle. As a young adult, I never knew my worth. I equated love with fleshly desires. As such, the adversary plotted to steal my destiny. He had already peaked into my future and saw the threat I would bring against his kingdom. So, he thought he had me after the death of my daughter and son, failed relationships, domestic violence, and insecurities.

Father God, thank You for my wilderness experience. You taught me how to dwell in the secret place of the most high. Every step taken in my dry places purged generational curses from my bloodline. My brokenness was healed and I received deliverance in my soul. Your footprint was all I could see manifested in the sand. I found refuge in You as my faith increased. The Holy Spirit illuminated elements of what "real love" and a relationship looks like.

Father God, I want others to experience "real love," which can only be found in You. Allow them to develop a more intimate relationship with You, which is the catalyst by which all of our relationships were created. When we return to You, our first love, all of our relationships will flourish, giving Your name all the glory. In Jesus' name.

Amen.

Reflective Scripture:
Psalm 91

Dr. Sonya V. Wade Johnson

LIFE WITHOUT LIFE

Dear God,

I thank You for my life and all You have richly blessed me with throughout the years. You have given me an abundance of blessings and I am beyond grateful. Lord, the desire of my heart is to be a mother. Your Word says that You will grant the desires of my heart, and my desire is to be a mother. Yet, my prayers have always been that I want to be in Your will for my life. So, God, since I submit to Your will, I will accept that Your will for my life is not to be a mother biologically. But, God, You have allowed me to be a mother and a role model to so many children. Even in this place, I never lost my praise to You and my hope is still in You. My heart's desire is to still do and be in Your will for my life. God, I know that the safest place to be is in Your will. But, without giving birth to life, allow me to remain whole and submissive to Your will and to stay in Your Word. Continue to guide me toward the path that You have ordained especially for me. Let my light shine in a way that others may see the work You are doing in me. Life is what You give, and I am grateful that

You have allowed my life, without life, to touch the lives of so many. God, I am grateful and will continue to be faithful. In Jesus' name, I thank You.

Amen.

Reflective Scripture:
Luke 1:45

Courtney Taylor

EXTENDING FORGIVENESS

Dear God,

This is probably one of the hardest things I have ever had to do. I ask You, oh Lord, to help me to take on Your character, so that I may extend the *love* and the *grace* to forgive those who have wronged me or caused me pain in such a way that I wanted to give up on life, throw in the towel, and completely lose focus on what You have called me to do here in the earth realm for Your kingdom purposes.

God, I ask that You help me to let go of any offences or past transgressions that try to weigh me down or keep me in a place of bitterness and stagnation. God, I release any form of unforgiveness, for my peace depends upon it. My ability to move forward depends upon it. My sanity depends upon it. My health depends upon it. My joy depends upon it. My ability to love and be free depends upon it. Dear Lord, help me to see that You are using all things for my good. God, I realize that I am not perfect. As You have forgiven me for *every* shortcoming, help me to forgive others.

Lord, grant me the strength to stand in adversity and to know that what does not kill me only makes me stronger. Help me to realize that every Judas experience was necessary for the greater good that's coming my way.

When I want to take revenge, vindicate me, Lord. Validate Your Word over my life. Humble me and help me to love my enemies and to do well towards them at all times.

Help me to forgive myself. Help me, God, to forgive in every possible way. Thank You in advance.

Amen.

Reflective Scripture:
Ephesians 4:32-5:2

Rev. Dr. Janie Dowdy-Dandridge, D Min.

GRIEVING COURAGEOUSLY: MY SON'S DEATH TAUGHT ME HOW TO MOURN

Dear God,

I come to You courageously and unapologetically as a grieving mother, like so many others who are suffering from the death of their children. Help us to accept what we cannot understand as life-threatening illnesses, violent crimes, acts of mayhem, homicides, and senseless suicides cause us to experience grief. Gracious God, grief is real but through it all, God, You sustained me. God, I pray for families grieving the loss of their children. I come to You, God, because I know You are familiar with grief. I come with renewed gratitude and thankfulness in my season of silence, separation, and discouragement. I pray for grieving mothers whose children died of untimely and unfortunate deaths. Oh God, help me to trust the process and to better understand how to be a companion to other mothers, grandmothers, aunts, and surrogate mothers. Help us to begin anew. I pray that we will find a resolve in Your plan for our lives as we mourn the grief we feel from the loss of our children. Eternal God, it's not always easy, but I thank You for Your sovereign presence.

When I thought it was too difficult to move on, in the serenity of silence, I heard Du'Juan's voice cheering me on from the balconies of Heaven, saying, "Mama, you can do this. You are an overcomer. Get up. Hey, Judy, you got this." Lord, may we find meaning and purpose for what is yet to come in our lives. Gracious God, as I grapple with life's uncertainties, help me to embrace the grief that will ultimately lead to healing, realizing it's okay not to be afraid of death.

"Remember, grief is a process not an event, it takes time."—Dr. Alan Wolfelt, *Understanding Your Grief*

Amen.

Reflective Scripture:
Psalm 147:3

HANDLING LEADERSHIP WITH PRAYER

Dear God,

Daily, I struggle with negative leadership news that threatens to upset the natural landscape of my life. Help me to be mindful of Jesus' words that say, "For our struggle is not against flesh and blood, but against rulers, against the authorities, against the powers of this dark world and against the spiritual forces of evil in the heavenly realms" (Ephesians 6:12; NIV). Forgive me, Lord, for not relying on Your Word. Instead, I joined the world's complaining pity party which affects my Christian witness. Let me not forget that through it all, Jesus never submitted to a pity party, but to the "nevertheless" will of God! Lord, I have been negligent in my call to remind others of Your warning that "In this world You shall have tribulation" (John 16:33a). When tribulations come, help me to count it all joy (James 1:2) for You are pruning me for a breakthrough to a greater worship, witness, and work in kingdom building.

From Genesis to Revelation, You teach me to handle life with the healing balm of prayer. As a good soldier of Jesus Christ, You exhort me to pray for all leadership that we might live a peaceful life that pleases You, our Savior. Quicken me to know that prayerlessness births unspiritual situations. Forgive me for not modeling Jesus' example on Calvary to pray for my offenders and forgive their sins.

Lord, keep me mindful that Your promises are fulfilled when I come boldly before the throne of grace and pray unceasingly. Strengthen me to handle leadership with prayer in the spirit of Jacob who said, "Lord, I will not let You go unless You bless me" (Genesis 32:26b). Lord, restore me, renew me, and revive me again! Because of Calvary, I pray this prayer in Jesus' name!

Amen.

Reflective Scripture:
1 Timothy 2:1-4

Rev. Dr. Sonja V. Brown Deloatch

A COVER OF LOVE

Dear God,

Throughout my life, I did not always know who You were, what You did, and why I needed You. It seemed to me that You would drift in and out of my life, leaving and forsaking me. I attended church each Sunday, and I was very actively involved. I was taught to pray as the disciples did, but I still could not find You. I realized that I had a gift to sing to glorify You. Yet, I did not know where to find You. Oh Lord, how I needed You. God, as I grew into a woman, I found myself still searching for an answer. Looking to be loved, needing to be loved, and longing for a spiritual covering. Lord God, I sought peace and a place like no other. I was alone, searching for you, Father!

Lord, I come on this day thanking You for being the ultimate Father to me. I prayed for Sundays to come each week so that I could learn more about You. Thank You for the formative years of my life. Thank You for the transformation that continues to groom and mold me. Learning that You never left or forsook me continues to be the covering I need. At each turn and twist of my life, You were always there providing just what I needed. I just needed to ask and not worry about the things of this world but be transformed. For the rest of my life, I will continue to praise You and strive for Your kingdom and glory. God, Your sweet voice that whispers in my ear; Your touch that holds me close and never lets me go. Thank You! You took away the bitterness and the loneliness that plagued my soul, and You replaced those things with Your loving kindness. For this and all things, I just want to say THANK YOU!

Amen.

Reflective Scripture:
Luke 12:28-31

Clara Matimba

IS IT TOO HARD TO LOVE UNCONDITIONALLY? TEACH ME, LORD!

Dear God,

Who am I to place limitations on loving the people around me? Am I perfect? I certainly do not think so! Lord, I have struggled with loving unconditionally because they did this and that to me, so why should I even love them? How can I claim to be a child of God, yet I struggle with loving others unconditionally? How quickly, Lord, You reminded me that You died on the cross for my sins and You redeemed it all. Teach me, Lord, to love others as You love me. That means loving others unconditionally. I seek unconditional love that does not see past or present hurt caused by others in any shape or form. I restrain my mind and my thoughts, and I tame my tongue regarding what I say about those who hurt me in any way. Teach me to understand that conditional love is rooted to unforgiveness in my heart. I will not suffocate anyone in my life with unforgiveness and judgment. If loving unconditionally becomes unhealthy, teach me, Lord, to gracefully walk away in love, because no one owes me anything. I owe it to myself to be at peace and love unconditionally from a distance.

Let my heart be content with You and You alone so that loving others unconditionally becomes a habit. Loving others unconditionally brings peace, elevation in my faith, calmness, restoration, unspeakable joy, and abundant blessings. I pray for Your presence. I need You every moment of my life because Your unconditional love sustains me and gives me new breath and mercies every morning. I will use the same measure to love others unconditionally.

Thank You, Lord, I have finally learned Your ultimate command to love others unconditionally. My faith is strengthened. I am blessed beyond measure. I have untouchable peace, unspeakable joy, and my walk with You is a living testimony. Unconditional love is inscribed on my heart now and forever. I thank You!

Amen.

Reflective Scripture:
1 Corinthians 13:4-7

Jahara Davis

A MOMENT WITHIN A SEASON OF RESTING IN PEACE

Dear God,

You created me. You set the divine purpose over my life to be the head and not the tail. I am Your child. I am asking for Your protection from all hurt, harm, and danger. At this very moment, I surrender my whole life to You. Over the course of a season, I prayed for long-lasting friendships. During that season, I became vulnerable and open. I truly believed Your will was being done as I formed relationships with those who I felt were meant to be a part of my life. I believed I was free to be myself without judgment. I believed Your light was shining internally and externally. I prayed for them, I sought them for advice, and I revealed my soul to them. I know now that it was only for a season. Lord, I was blinded by how Your children felt about me. I endured the lies and the fabrications told about me that put a stain on my character as a friend, mother, woman, and a child of God. I am demanding for You to fix this.

I have not been a perfect child, and for that I am sorry. I am standing on Your Word that guides me and leads me to who I will become and where I am destined to be. In order for me to become that person and to continue to walk down the path You have set for me, I forgive those who have mistreated me. I am no longer concerned about Your children. I am using faith, the size of a mustard seed, for You to move this mountain. It no longer requires my energy, space, and time, because it is not like You. This season is for resting in peace.

Amen.

Reflective Scripture:
Matthew 17:20

Leroy Francis Jr.

PRESSING PAST A PARENT'S PAIN TO PRISON

Dear God,

I come to You as humbly as I know how, broken and in pieces. God, You are the giver of life and we are Yours to do with as You wish. My desire is to always be in Your presence, for without You I am nothing. God, You know us inside and out. You know all of our thoughts before You awake us on a new day. You knew the job You would have my son to do in this life's journey. You call him servant, I call him Jeremy Matthew Francis, but the State of Texas calls him 1913681. Father, at times I feel as though I've failed him even though You give us our own free will and our decisions come with a price. Jeremy is now paying the price—a life sentence without the possibility of parole.

BUT GOD!

No matter what the court says, You sit high and Your grasp is undeniable. God, I just have to stay out of Your way and watch You work this out. God, You kept Your arms around me when the verdict was read and the jailers took him away. I just don't believe that this is how the story ends. You could have taken him from this earth 17 years prior, but

You saw fit to place him where he has no other options but to hear, believe, and submit to Your will.

As the father waited on the prodigal son to return home and upon his arrival all were reunited, I ask for Your guidance on this journey and for my family to have comfort in knowing that You have it all under control because You are the author and finisher of this story. I thank You in advance for whatever You so desire.

Amen.

Reflective Scripture:
Luke 15:11-32

Sherry Wurgler

MY SAVIOR, MY REDEEMER, MY HOPE AND JOY

Dear God,

Thank You for being my hope and salvation through those times when all around me seemed to threaten my very survival. You were there in the middle of my disbelief, in the midst of my pain, and in the middle of all that was wrong. You were there in the midst of my doubt and uncertainty. You gave me strength and courage to live through it all. You gave me the strength to not give up. You were my source of compassion and love when all seemed hopeless.

I felt Your presence, Your love, Your protection, Your compassion, and Your strength; they permeated every ounce of my being. You filled my heart, soul, and mind with gratitude and love. Gratitude and a positive attitude give my life meaning, passion, and purpose. You were and will always be my source of courage, freedom, resilience, and love. You are my peace, my joy, my everything. I was renewed by Your grace and love.

God, You are my all in all. You are my everything when I feel doubt and uncertainty comes knocking on my door. You are my peace when my soul feels restless. You are my joy in the middle of sadness and grief.

I thank You for being steadfast and never failing. You are my guidance and source of direction when I feel lost. You fill me up when the world leaves me feeling empty and incomplete.

Amen.

Reflective Scripture:
2 Timothy 1:7

Charmaine Roots Castillo

CONTENDING FOR PEACE

Dear God,

I am still waiting for answers concerning the death of my child. Help me to walk in peace in the midst of the greatest storm of my life. Hold me steady as I cling to the knowledge that You are working all things out for my good. As I set my heart to believe Your promises, let me lay aside the disappointment that sometimes bleeds into my thoughts. In those lonely moments when sadness and hopelessness try to creep in and overtake me and the tears come, give me the courage that I need to continue to fight the good fight of faith, even through the pain.

God, I acknowledge that You have always been faithful and even as I cast the care of my waiting and broken heart onto You, remind me that I don't need to be anxious about the outcome, but that I can look to You—no matter what. As I make my requests known to You, thank You for comforting me by Your Spirit and perfecting the things that concern me.

Thank You for peaceful nights of sleep and helping me to use the peace that I find in You as a guide for each new day of my life. Thank You for the new mercies that greet me every morning. As I follow the sound of Your peace, help me to be still and know that You are God. When grief and questions begin to swirl in my mind, infuse my heart and soul with a peace that passes all understanding. As I receive Your peace, let me be a conduit of that peace so that I may in turn comfort others. Thank You for helping me.

Amen.

Reflective Scripture:
Genesis 41:16

I AM MORE THAN ENOUGH

Dear God,

Psalm 139:14 says that I am fearfully and wonderfully made and that my soul knoweth right well. I know Your Word is true. Help me, Lord, to apply it to my life. I've spent so much time comparing myself to others. I've spent time believing that I wasn't good enough and that I didn't measure up. The words I heard during my childhood have left me scarred. The abuses I witnessed and endured in my home have left me broken. God, the hurts afflicted by others that I could not address because of fear have left me confused about who I am and why You created me. The stigma of divorce, and the feelings of abandonment and rejection have left me bitter and untrusting.

Oh God! Because of these things, I'm insecure. I pretend for others that I'm okay. I wear a mask so no one can see my insecurities. This mask helps me grin and smile as the poet says. The mask of fashion, the latest hairstyles, and a high-powered career are all so that I can pretend for others. Only You see the crack in my armor. Only You see the tears that slip down my cheeks when no one is looking. But today, I come into Your presence stating that I'm not okay, and I need Your help. Help me to truly understand that I am Your righteousness. Help me to truly understand that I am part of the beloved of Christ. Help me to know that everything You created is good. And because it's good, I can hold my head high and no longer feel inferior or walk in bitterness. Help me, Lord, to know that I am more than enough.

Amen.

Reflective Scripture:
Psalm 139:14

Larry C. Brown

LIVING A LIE—SPEAKING THE TRUTH ABOUT THIS WORLD WE LIVE IN

Dear God,

I want to thank You for making me the person I am today. I apologize for the shortcomings I have had in my life. Me knowing You, Lord, kept my heart in the right place. I have been walking around in this world trying to satisfy the people around me. I gave my life to them just to make them happy. My heart knew it was wrong, but my mind and body loved what was going on. When I go to church on Sundays, I give You all the praise and glory. The messages I write are true words from the heart that tell people how to give their lives to You, Jesus Christ. But, I was not living the life I was speaking. Lord, I ask that You direct my mind to go along with my heart so that I can always praise You and feel no shame. Help me to understand the truth about serving You. I must give my all to You. Forgive me, Lord, for my wrong-doings.

I am here as Your child needing Your power. I am fighting to live my life according to Your will in this world. Sometimes I think that I must live a lie in order to survive in this world. God, I just want to say thank You for not letting me fall into the ways of this troubled world. Thank You for controlling my destiny. Lord, You are the Almighty God and You can take my troubled mind and put it at ease. With the world after my soul, I give my heart to You so that it can be purified. Lord, when I turn to You, my mind turns away from this troubled world that is trying to take over my soul. With my hand in Your hand, Lord, I feel I will do no wrong.

Thank You, Jesus Christ, for forgiving me.

Amen.

Reflective Scripture:
Proverbs 21:1-4

Sharla Thomas

PRAYER FOR THE HEALING AND STRENGTH OF A SICK CHILD

Dear God,

I pray for my child who is living with a rare disease. I'm thankful for the life of my son whom You gave to me. I know You to be a God of healing and restoring. I pray for healing and comfort daily for all suffering with this disease. God, You are all-knowing and all-seeing. You created my son in Your likeness and image. I believe You to be a God of faithfulness; a God that does exceedingly and abundantly above all.

When my son is sick and in pain, God please grant him comfort and peace. Give him strength to rely on the Scriptures that he knows—that by Your strips he is healed—and help him to remember that You will never leave or forsake him. God, strengthen us as parents as we watch our child endure this illness. When we as parents feel weak and overwhelmed, encourage us to remember that we never walk alone. In the times we think we are alone, You are right there. You are the same God yesterday, today, and forevermore. The same miracle that You performed for the woman with the issue of blood, You will perform for my son.

God, grant every medical professional that cares for my son the resilience and knowledge to treat his disease. Grant the medical research professionals the strength, stamina, and understanding to continually study for a cure. God, You gave us a rare son whom we are thankful for every day. We give him back to You and trust You for a healing. We give You all of the praise and the glory.

Amen.

Reflective Scripture:
Matthew 15:28

Keith L. Maddox

FATHER TO FATHER

Dear God,

You might kill me, but I have no other hope. I am going to argue my case with You. Job 13:15. I am frustrated and angry. Lord, I serve You and I preach for You. I lay hands on those who are sick and I watch them recover. As Your servant, I have seen You break fevers and straighten the mouths of people who have had strokes. Yet, I have prayed for 25 years, asking You to heal my daughter from neurofibromatosis, and the answer seems delayed. Is there a purpose or a plan for her? Where is the good in this disease when it affects her physically, mentally, and emotionally? Yet, with tears and a heavy heart, I continue to submit to the power of Your name, knowing that Your name is higher than any other name. So, I ask again.

I pray by the authority of Your name, Jesus, that neurofibromatosis will surrender to the power of Your blood. I speak to the pain and the tumors that grow on her nerve fibers and cover her entire body, and I command you to CEASE and DESIST, in Jesus' name! God, You said that death and life are in the power of the tongue, so my daughter will be whole. She will have a long life. I ask that You satisfy her and show her Your salvation. Father, I speak to the depression that tries to attach itself to her and our family. I curse it from the root, in the name of Jesus. Touch, heal, and deliver. Now unto the King eternal, immortal, and invisible; to the only wise God our Savior be majesty, glory, dominion, and power, now and forevermore, in Jesus' name. It is DONE!

Amen.

Reflective Scripture:
Psalm 61:2

Camille McKenzie

LORD, MY LIFE IS YOUR BLANK SLATE!

Dear God,

All I can see now is darkness. I saw my loved one in every stage of my life. It is hard for me to believe that he/she is gone, and I will not see him/her again.

I don't know how I will live without him/her I have nowhere else to go, God, but to You. My heart is broken, Lord, and I know that You are near to the brokenhearted. Be near to me now. Help me to sense Your presence. Save me, Lord. Heal my heart. I am in so much pain.

Here's my life. I give it to You. My life is now Your blank slate to write on it whatever You want. I confess to You that I have no other plans. I can't see past this moment or past this pain that I am feeling.

You have asked me to put my trust in You. Please give me the grace to trust You in these dark days of my life. Help me to believe and cling to Your promise that You will do something new in my life and that a way will be made in all this darkness that now surrounds me.

Lord, I cry out to You because I keep remembering the past, my former life with my loved one. It is hard for me to focus on the promise of a future life that will be blessed

without him/her. Lord, I believe, but help my unbelief! Thank You that despite how I feel now, brighter days are ahead.
Amen.

Reflective Scripture:
Isaiah 43:18-19

Ernetta Caldwell

LORD, PLEASE FILL ME UP, I AM RUNNING ON EMPTY!

Dear God,

I want to thank You for allowing me to see this day. I know that as long as I have breath in my body, You still have plans for my life! I am so grateful for all that You have done for me and my family and all that You are going to do. I ask that as I am running on empty that You fill me up with Your Word, strength, and endurance. As I am obedient to help lead others to You, help me to keep pressing forward when I feel empty. I know that self-care is important and taking care of my temple should come first. Help me to know that saying no to others is not a sin and help me to always say yes to Your purpose and the plans You have for me. Help me not to grow weary in well doing but to surrender my will for Yours. The day-to-day can become so busy but help me not to forget to put You first in all that I do. Remove any distractions that can derail me from my purpose. Help me to stay focused on the dreams and goals You have given me. In the times that I feel I don't have strength, please remind me that You are my strength and "I can do all things through Christ who strengthens me" (Philippians 4:13; NKJV). As I intercede in prayer for others (my lost son, those hurting, and family members), help me not to lose faith in Your Word. As I pour into others, please send others that can pour into me. Lord, I cannot be all that You called me to be if I am empty. I thank You for filling me up.

In Jesus' name.

Amen.

Reflective Scripture:
Matthew 4:4

Scott Wilson

SOMETIMES IT IS THE SIMPLE PRAYERS THAT ARE LIFE CHANGING

Dear God,

"God, I don't want to die, but I don't know how to live. Help me."

After I said that prayer over four years ago, God sent people across my path that changed the course of my life. This past year, I was humbled and honored to be asked by our former police chief, Mac Tristan, to attend Danny Barton's swearing in ceremony as the new police chief for Coppell, Texas.

As Danny's sons removed his old emblems and pinned the new stars on his shirt, and his wife pinned his new badge on his chest, all I could think was: "Out with the old and in with the new." Or, as Danny phrased it more eloquently, "A new chapter begins, built on the previous chapters of life that led to this point, and I can't do it alone."

The men and women of the CPD were there when I was at my worst. When I was completely broken and unlovable. Despite that they showed me respect, kindness, and grace, none of which I had earned on November 13, 2015. I was just another drunk arrested for my second DWI with a .40 BAC.

God had other plans for the next chapter He was writing in my life. Through my journey of jail, rehab, a 12-step program, baptism in the north fork of the Guadalupe River, and making amends for my past, it led to Danny and I being good friends, and Mac becoming one of my business partners.

God set my path in a new direction that started with a simple, honest prayer from a broken man to now a grateful, recovered alcoholic. Sometimes it is the most simple and honest prayer that leads to a life changing direction.

"God, I don't want to die, but I don't know how to live. Help me."

Amen.

Reflective Scripture:
Jeremiah 29:11

PETITIONING GOD, BY FAITH, TO MOVE MY MOUNTAINS

Dear God,

I have mountains before me. I seek You, Lord! I am reminded that You are Alpha and Omega, the beginning and the end. You are my Father, Adonai the Sovereign Lord over all things. God, You are full of goodness, faithfulness, and power. Everywhere I turn it seems like there is a mountain in my way. Therefore, I put my hope in You in every area of my life, knowing that I should call on You and not trust in myself. Lord, I am petitioning You to move the mountain(s) of _____ (sickness, pain, a broken marriage, unhealthy relationships, debt, unemployment, or parenting a difficult or special needs child). Through faith, I know that it is only You that can bless, heal, move and destroy my mountain(s). Lord, please hear my prayer and take over; I willingly take a back seat.

God, I need Your favor, guidance, and miracles right now. Lord, where people are saying "No," I am trusting You to move mountains and say "Yes!" God, Your Word says that I can ask anything according to Your will and You will hear me. If I believe I have received it, then I shall have the very thing that I am asking for (1 John 5:14-15). I thank You, God, for

being a way maker and mountain mover! I thank You, God, for interceding on my behalf and bringing me to a point of blessing, healing, and restoration in my life. I thank You, God, for hearing the petitions of my heart and reminding me that I can trust in Your Word. I have full faith in You to be the God You say You are and to give me the victory! In Jesus' name.
Amen.

Reflective Scripture:
Mark 11:22-24

Kim Coles

THESE FOUR WORDS

Dear God,

Yes. Please. More and Thank You.
 Amen.
 I learned this simple prayer in September 2019 during my epic trip to Egypt. I was so excited to be on that trip with women from five different countries. All of us were believers, but the group was made up of several different faiths. When our trip leader shared this simple prayer that we all could share in together, we were thrilled.
 "Yes. Please. More and Thank You."
 I immediately resonated with the simplicity *and* complexity of those words. You see, I've never considered myself a "good" prayer. Meaning, I don't feel very comfortable praying in public because I just don't know what to say.
 I can never remember the longer ritualistic prayers that require memorization, like when I attended Lutheran school from grades K-8, and later when my father became an Episcopal priest. I just couldn't keep up with all the answer and callbacks.
 When I pray, it has always been a very private, quiet, and personal experience. I just talk to the Creator whenever and however I want. On a walk. On a plane. While

waiting to book a gig. While waiting for my date to call for a second date!

I'm generally conversational with God. I say thank You and amen at the end and that is my only constant.

Yet, with those four words, I now feel powerful and protected. I can customize my prayers for what I really want to say every time!

Yes- I am open to where the Creator would have me go and what is expected of me. Yes, I will seize opportunities to see the lessons.

Please- Send me the resources that I need to be a better person and serve more. Please make me stronger and protect me.

More love. More peace. More truth. More joy. More prosperity. More health. More wisdom.

Thank You for all of it. For waking me up each day. Thank You for the great lessons that make me the best version of me.

"Yes. Please. More and Thank You" makes me feel connected and that is what touches my soul the most.

Amen.

Reflective Scripture:
Colossians 4:2

About the Authors

Dr. Pasha Carter took a $500.00 investment and turned it into a multi-million-dollar empire. She is one of America's most influential direct sales leaders and is ranked among the top 15 female networkers in the world out of over 14 million women worldwide.

When Dr. Dennis Kimbro and The Napoleon Hill Foundation interviewed 100 of America's Wealthiest African Americans for *The Wealth Choice*, Pasha was interviewed alongside Steve Harvey, Tyler Perry, T.D. Jakes, and other influential leaders.

She is currently on the expert panel of *Forbes* magazine where she writes articles and lends her business advice to CEOs, entrepreneurs, and influencers around the world.

Pasha has been featured in *Forbes* magazine, *Rolling Out*, *Influential People Magazine*, *Sheen Magazine*, *MizCEO* magazine, and *SUCCESS From Home Magazine* to name a few.

Her passion is seeing people break through the financial bondage and excuses that stop them from reaching their true potential.

Learn more at www.PashaCarter.com

Tiffany Easley, Soar Strategist, is helping others soar into the life of their dreams. Through her signature Soar Program, she shows others how to recognize the power of their dreams and visions, maximize the results of their initiatives, and successfully launch their projects.

Through her signature Soar Program, she teaches others how to create a platform of power, purpose, and positioning while influencing them to tap into their resilience to never give up.

In addition to being a Soar Strategist, Tiffany is also an advocate, author, coach, and a John Maxwell Team certified speaker. She is known for her passionate, energetic, and practical approach to reaching entrepreneurs, women, and faith-based leaders.

Learn more at www.tiffanyreasley.com

Russell M. Williamson Sr. is a believer, husband, father, executive, entrepreneur, and a former franchise owner. Russell is a results-driven and transformational leader, a change agent, and an effective communicator. He is a best-selling author and has been featured in *Dallas Morning News, Dallas Business Journal, D Magazine's D Healthcare Daily* as a contributing editor, and *NY Sales, Marketing and Media* where he also graced the cover of the magazine.

Russell is acclaimed for leadership development and for coaching individuals and teams to reach peak performance. He is a graduate of the U.S. Military Academy at West Point and has degrees from Troy University, the Wharton School of the University of Pennsylvania, and Southern Methodist University. Russell has won numerous awards as a combat Veteran and in business. He has been married for 27 years to his wife, Cheryl, and has three children and two grandchildren.

To connect, email him at Russwill@924sports.com

Brenda Anderson Parker, BS, MS, is a powerful, dynamic, spirit filled author and speaker, who is respected for her ability to captivate, motivate, and inspire audiences to make immediate changes in their lives by being the best that they can be. She encourages others to live life to its fullest. Her assignment is to impact the kingdom with the Word of God in an excellent way.

Brenda has a bachelor of science degree in business administration and a master of science in human relations and business. She is the author of *The Lessons of Chelby*, a book about her granddaughter who had her first of five strokes at 19 months. Brenda's book is for individuals dealing with life's challenges. Brenda's audiences say things like, "She's inspiring, enthusiastic, and confident," "Brenda's messages are stimulating and thought-provoking," "She's just real," "Her enthusiasm is contagious," and, "We want her back."

To connect, email her at baparker3@aol.com

Dr. Betty Burroughs Speaks, The Extraordinaire, is an award-winning I Change Nations Black Belt Speaker, Army Veteran, celebrity publicist for The National Quartet, ambassador to The Veteran Woman, LLC, global network virtual marketer and entrepreneur, seven-time bestselling contributing author, Jesus Woman at Godheads Ministry, ambassador to the Pink Pulpit Ministry, and master storyteller. She also coordinates publicity events and handles multiple clients.

Dr. Betty assists and guides individuals and couples through their personal and professional challenges by providing faith-based mentorship and designing an individualized plan that will propel them into their God-given purpose!

With over 20 years of military experience, over 15 years in multiple avenues of ministry, and over 25 years of marriage while raising a blended family, her extensive educational background and experience provides her with the tools to design a plan that will have you living intentionally to create the life of your dreams.

Learn more at www.bettyspeaks.com

Dr. Onika L. Shirley, known as Dr. O, is the founder and CEO of Action Speaks Volume, Inc. an international confidence and anti-procrastination strategist, motivational speaker, and Christian counselor. She is also the founder and director of Action Speaks Volume Orphanage Home in India and founder and director of Action Speaks Volume Sewing School in Pakistan. Recently, Dr. O partnered with Bayfu Children's Orphanage Home in Uganda. She was blessed to have coaching clients all the way in Namibia, Africa. She is an author, master storyteller, radio host of Action Takers Walking by Faith live radio broadcast, and a serial entrepreneur.

Dr. O is a biological mother, adoptive mother, foster mother, and proud grandmother to baby Aubrey. Of all things Dr. O does, she is most proud of her profound faith in Christ and her opportunity to serve the body of Christ globally. She impacts the lives of many around the world.

Learn more at www.actionspeaksvolum.com

Katrice Gray is a Newark, New Jersey, native currently residing in Raleigh, North Carolina. Katrice graduated from Mount Saint Mary's Academy in Watchung, New Jersey, and received her B.S. in business management from Shaw University in Raleigh, North Carolina. For over twenty years, her corporate career ranged from top seller for major companies to corporate trainer facilitating the industries in grooming the best talent for sales and marketing teams. In 2014, Katrice left the corporate structure for law enforcement and became a part of the Wake County Sheriff's Office. Her passion for beautifying keeps her busy upcycling furniture and decorating spaces for her clients. Katrice's goal is to use the barriers she's had to overcome to help others recognize why we are "Broken to Be Made Whole."

Katrice is a 30-year member of Alpha Kappa Alpha Sorority, Inc., and the proud mother of one son, Brandon J. Gray, who is a Veteran of the United States Air Force.

To connect, email her at KatriceGray@hotmail.com

Dr. Peggie Etheredge Johnson is a seasoned pastor's wife; author of *Kingdom Of Pearls: Recovering The Wounded Heart*; co-author of *Soulful Prayers, When CEOs Pray,* and *Business Principles For The Beauty CEO*. She is passionate about the spiritually abused, the marginalized, and impoverished children and families. She is an adjunct instructor at Columbia International University, owner of Kingdom Of Pearls, LLC, independent Mary Kay beauty consultant, cosmetologist, certified Bible teacher, certified life coach, seminar/workshop curriculum designer/leader, blogger, and motivational speaker.

Dr. Johnson is the lead instructor of Marketplace Bible Study, director of women's and children's ministries, and cross-cultural missions' leader. She is married to Bishop Richard Johnson, they have three sons, two daughters-in-love, and five adorable grandchildren.

Dr. Johnson earned a B.A. at W.L. Bonner College, M.A. and M.Ed. at Columbia International University, and an EdD at Capella University.

Learn more at www.mykingdompearls.com

Tiffany Mayfield is a renowned and award-winning tax franchise owner, personal and business tax professional, and bestselling author. Although passionate about many things, Tiffany's calling is to authentically and fearlessly motive women to unleash their best life, recreate their story, change the script, and become their own superhero through faith. She believes that change isn't free; it will cost your old life and your old life will pay the down payment on the road to your purpose.

Ms. Mayfield's extraordinary story of recreating her own life while recovering from devastating heartbreak after heartbreak transformed her mindset to help her become the ultimate change and superhero she longed to discover.

Tiffany believes every woman possesses the power to overcome learned behaviors and negative mindsets. She believes that through strong faith, prayer, tools, and resources, the empowered woman can embark upon a new standard of clarity and perspective and recognize the power in her strength.

To connect, email her at tiffany@themayfieldfirm.com

Alisa Allen is a certified etiquette instructor. Her company has enlightened individuals on the importance of etiquette (corporate, dining, and protocol).

Alisa works for one of the largest telecommunications companies in the world, AT&T, where she has been for 24 years. She has a B.A. degree from Texas Woman's University and an MBA from Amberton University.

Alisa received the Social Action Award from Phi Beta Sigma Fraternity, Inc. for her work with the Sigma Beta Boys Club. She has received the President's Volunteer Service Award for the past 12 years. In 2018, she presented at the Alpha Kappa Alpha Sorority, Inc. International Conference, the Black Women's Expo in Dallas, Texas, and was named the Dallas Black Chamber of Commerce's 2018 recipient of the Connie Roseborough Volunteer of the Year Award. Alisa also received the 2019 Etiquette Instructor of the Year Award from the board of the National Association of Urban Etiquette Professionals.

To connect, email her at
Yourpresenceisimportant@gmail.com

Dr. Eric L. Holmes is a senior coordinator in the otolaryngology department at Johns Hopkins Hospital in Baltimore, Maryland. His fervor to excel and push his abilities has led him to earn an impressive number of awards at Johns Hopkins such as: the Edward Halle Award, the Martin Luther King Award, the Radiology Customer Service Award (for two years), and the Employee of the Year Award.

With a passion and dedication to further his education and help others through his teachings, Dr. Holmes has earned a bachelor's and master's degree in biblical studies and theology, and a master's and doctorate degree in Christian education at North Carolina College of Theology. He has also been featured in *The Writers Live* newsletter published by the Enoch Pratt Library Compass. In addition, his book, *The Power of the Seed*, is now available in the Enoch Pratt Libraries, the Baltimore County Libraries, and Dauphin County Libraries in Pennsylvania.

To connect, email him at elynnk1306@gmail.com

Juanita Payne was born in Jamaica, Queens, New York. She has a bachelor's in computer systems, a master's in internet security, and a master's in cyber security. Juanita also graduated from the Institute of Integrative Nutrition (IIN) as a certified health coach. Juanita has two bestselling co-author accolades as a writer in *Beyond Her Reflection* and *Soulful Prayers*.

A dedicated woman of God, Juanita has stayed strong and is a beacon of light for her three children. She also owns Juanita's Crown Creations, an at-home salon operating with the idea of helping all women become greater versions of themselves. As a self-taught, now licensed braiding aficionado, Juanita has given confidence to many women for over 40 years. In her never-ending pursuit of personal freedom, financial expansion, and progressive thinking, Juanita plans to continue influencing the world through her connection with God, and thriving in eternal love.

To connect, email her at chose2bchosn@gmail.com

Marsha Taylor has been an educator for over twenty years. She is passionate and committed to being a catalyst and advocate for children to excel academically, physically, spiritually, and holistically. She has developed a wealth of knowledge and experience within the church. Her calling is to empower, motivate, and encourage all people who come into contact with her to be their best self by changing their mindset.

After earning her teaching degree, Mrs. Taylor went on to earn her bachelor's in guidance and counseling at The Institute for Theological Leadership Development while living in Jamaica, her native country. Shortly after, she migrated to the United States as a teacher ambassador. She later completed her master's degree in educational leadership at Regent University in Virginia.

Mrs. Taylor currently lives in North Carolina where she continues to serve in the field of education and is presently working on developing a program to narrow the reading gap for brown kids.

To connect, email her at Marshataylor583@gmail.com

Tammy L. Woodard is a multi-bestselling author and transformational speaker dedicated to helping others discover their gifts and reach their full potential. She is also the owner of Woodard Worldwide Visions, LLC.

Tammy received her bachelor's in 1992 at Shaw University and her master's in 2016 at University of Maryland University College. She is a Silver Star member of Alpha Kappa Alpha Sorority, Inc. Tammy is also the visionary author of the anthology, *Beyond Her Reflections*, and was the recipient of the Co-author of the Year Award at the 2018 Indie Author Legacy Awards for her collaborative efforts as co-author in the book, *Soul Talk*, released in 2017. Also, Tammy previously served as the co-manager of the Cheryl Brand Ambassador Program for Williamson Media Group, LLC, and Cheryl Polote Williamson, LLC.

Tammy resides in Fort Mill, South Carolina, and is the proud mother of two sons, Thomas Jr. and Damahje, and grandmother to her granddaughter Skylar.

To connect, email her at Designedpurposely@yahoo.com

Dee Bowden founded BCS Solutions, a revenue recovery company, from a personal desire to see small businesses make big-money impact. Dee believes small businesses fall prey to revenue loss because of poor accounting strategies. That's why she's on a mission to help them grow their financial bottom line by sharing her five-step program to revenue recovery. In fact, with over 20 years of financial experience, Dee has collected over $50 million for several companies and government agencies.

A graduate of Cambridge College, with a master's degree in management, the Boston native has spread her message on money management by appearing on many nationally recognized podcasts and at the 2019 Success Women's Conference that featured Iyanla Vanzant and Gloria Mayfield Banks.

Along with her success in financial management, Dee was featured in *Black Enterprise* magazine in the article "Sealing the Money Leaks: 5 Ways to Secure Your Cash Flow."

Learn more at www.bcsconsultinggrp.com

Dr. John Dandridge is a servant, husband, father, grandfather, brother, friend, educator, entrepreneur, and executive director. Reared under the auspices of the Air Force, he is also a highly decorated retired Army combat officer. As a preacher, pastor, and counselor, he fights spiritual and natural battles daily. He climbed steep mountains and crossed wide river valleys to be where he is today—a place of blissful awe and reflection.

As a change agent addressing Veterans concerns, Dr. John asked God one simple question: "What else do You still expect me to do?" God answered: "Teach others how to overcome hurdles and attain goals, and how to exercise self-care regularly and feel renewed. Above all, teach about good godly living now."

So, how will he answer this call to serve? He endeavors to establish the Dandridge Leadership Renewal Institute. Stay tuned!

Learn more at www.facebook.com/dandridgenhcd

Marlo Mozee, visionary and CEO of The Mansions on Park Row, is a mother of two, an entrepreneur, a licensed cosmetologist, a mentor to children and adults, a fashion lover, evangelist, pastor, and radio personality, host of the *Mornings at The Mansion* show on Blog Talk Radio, Facebook Live. She is also host and executive producer of *The Queendom Talk Show* on Roku TV.

Marlo always knew that she would be an entrepreneur, even while working for corporate America for over 35 years in upper management. Marlo takes pride in helping others fulfill their dreams, desires, and goals. She is an atmosphere changer and was a recipient of the 2015 NAACP Most Influential Women in Business Award. As the founder of New Wine Empowerment and Inspiration Group, and birther of Marlo Mozee Ministries and The Bling of the Earth Annual Women's Conference, Marlo lives by the mantra, "Come as You Are, and Leave With Purpose."

Learn more at www.marlomozeeministries.org

Symonia A. Montgomery is a woman with a passion to empower others. As an ordained pastor, poet, spoken word artist, motivational speaker, author, certified life coach, business owner, and founder of the non-profit organization, Girl Me Too, Symonia uses every platform to reach those in broken places. With a loving but stern disposition, she pushes people beyond their comfort level into their greatness. With 12 published works under her belt, Symonia has been featured on television, on the radio, in magazines and news-papers, and she has appeared in countless anthologies.

Symonia currently hosts a yearly women's retreat and youth poetry contest. She also gifts the Rosie Williams Scholarship, the Diamond Flower Award, the Love Mirror Award, and the Godsend Award yearly. She believes that helping others is a gift that keeps on giving. This mother of two has a bachelor's degree in accounting and a master's degree in strategic management with a focus in finance.

To connect, email her at yesgirlmetoo@aol.com

Debra Dibble Boone is a grateful believer in Jesus Christ. She is a recently retired professional who has worked in various engineering and managerial positions. Debra earned a bachelor of science degree in mechanical engineering from Prairie View A&M University in Prairie View, Texas. She has worked as a petroleum, manufacturing, and civil engineer in the private and public sectors, including executive level managerial positions.

Debra is an active member in church ministries and philanthropic organizations—serving in communities to cultivate and motivate youth in seeking higher education and assisting disadvantaged families and individuals in improving and sustaining successful lifestyles.

Debra is now focusing on entrepreneurial pursuits that will allow her to provide equity in employment for minorities and women in STEM related careers.

Debra and her husband Douglas reside in Austin, Texas, and enjoy golfing and traveling.

To connect, email her at debdib1908@gmail.com

Jessica L. Howard is a woman with a passion to serve. She was born and raised in Springfield, Massachusetts, the birthplace of basketball, and attended the University of Massachusetts Amherst, where she studied business and marketing. She has 10 years of experience in the healthcare insurance and consumer lending industries combined.

Jessica's church home is Mt. Zion Baptist Community Church in Springfield, Massachusetts. While there, she served as co-ministry leader of Get Connected, a ministry designed to fellowship with visitors and members through church and community events.

Jessica has a strong desire for entrepreneurship. She is also a natural hair enthusiast who loves to cook and travel. In 2018, she relocated to Dallas, Texas, and plans to start a family with the love of her life.

Jessica believes every experience has a divine purpose and encourages others to remember that "the struggle is part of your story, but the victory is for God's glory!"

To connect, email her at OWNlyJessbecause@gmail.com

Loni P. Pride is a loving wife and mother. She has a heart and passion to serve which is why she received her bachelor's degree in human services and her master's degree in social work. Loni currently operates as a prophetic intercessor at her local church. She believes in exemplifying the love of Christ and she views prayer as an essential part of her spiritual relationship with Him. Prayer allows her to communicate, petition, intercede, connect, and form intimacy and purification with the Lord. Her faith and prayers have opened doors, not only for her but for those on whose behalf she intercedes.

Loni loves to dance prophetically, act, travel, and apply her creativity to whatever she encounters. She desires to be a light by embracing others, lending a helping hand, praying, worshiping, encouraging, and being a true servant and leader. Loni's prayer is that marriages will be built not devoured.

To connect, email her at lonipride@yahoo.com

Sonya M. Hall-Brown is a wife, mother of five, and grand-mother of five. She has unmasked her truth and is dedicated to letting single parents know that their life is not ruined because they have children out of wedlock.

Sonya was born in Bronx, New York, and relocated to Blackstock, South Carolina. She received her degree from Columbia Junior College. She is the founder, owner, and CEO of L and S Cleaning Express, LLC, (established in 2015) which has since been renamed Dusting Destiny in memorial of their daughter. She is an active member of St. Luke Baptist Church in Winnsboro, South Carolina, where she is a youth advisor, trustee, and assistant financial secretary.

Sonya was honored to serve as a Cheryl Brand Ambassador in 2018. She published her first written work in the anthology, *Beyond Her Reflections*, a 2018 Amazon bestseller. She has since become a two-time, bestselling author; adding the Amazon bestseller, *Soulful Prayers*, to her ministry.

To connect, email her at smbrown1226@live.com

D'Adriewne Pickett is the founder of Re-Inventing Yourself Consultation where she counsels, mentors, and coaches people of all ages through their change process. D'Adriewne has worked with clients five years of age and older. Her specialty is working with families, women, and children. She assists them in realizing their value and worth, and empowers each person she encounters to gain a greater understanding of the part they play in their personal journey. She inspires those she works with to do the personal work in their transformation.

D'Adriewne embraces both traditional and non-traditional forms of counseling, such as aroma in therapy, music in therapy, energy release, drama, and play in therapy. D'Adriewne assists clients in realizing that life is a personal journey; a day-to-day adventure to discover who they are and the legacy they want to leave behind.

To connect, email her at gdstldo@gmail.com

Jennifer Harris Nyanfor is a motivational speaker and a certified innovative life coach. Jennifer is the owner of J's Creative Marketing, a marketing company that provides a variety of services including marketing strategies; business plans; fisher of men leadership training; and innovative life coaching to businesses, colleges, and churches. Jennifer has over 20 years of experience in business, management, leadership, and organizational development.

Jennifer has dual associate degrees in business management and marketing from Midland Technical College. She has a bachelor of science degree in organizational leadership from Columbia International University, a master of business administration degree from Southern Wesleyan University, and she is currently pursuing a doctoral degree in business administration with a specialization in strategy and innovation.

Jennifer is the mother of two sons, 16-year-old Arthur B. Nyanfor II and 26-year-old Rhys B. Nyanfor. She also has a daughter-in-law, Shelly Nyanfor, and a granddaughter, Naomi Jennifer Nyanfor.

Learn more at www.jscreativemarketing-llc.com

Linda D. Lee is the CEO of LL Media Group, LLC, a personal development consultancy company. She is a professional certified life coach (PCLC), certified Christian mentor (CCM), international speaker, and bestselling author. She is the recipient of the 2019 Indie Author Legacy Awards Author of the Year (Relationships). Linda has amassed 22 years of combined experience in personal development and emotion management strategies.

As a Family Relationship Midwife®, her mission is to build healthy relationships using biblical principles while transforming mindsets. Linda teaches entrepreneurs how to turn their pain into purposeful tools using sustainability plans. Her assignments extend from the United States to Ghana, Africa; London, the United Kingdom; and Dubai, UAE.

As a prolific writer, she has been labeled "a powerhouse phenomenon" by *Huffington Post*. Linda has appeared on international platforms such as: STARR Radio UK, KHVN Heaven 97, *MizCEO* magazine, *The Sherry Bronson Show*, ROKU TV, and more.

Learn more at www.1lindadlee.com

Dr. Sonya V. Wade Johnson is an educator in Nashville, Tennessee. She has served the school district for the past 22 years as a teacher and numeracy coach. She is responsible for providing professional development to teachers so that student achievement increases and teacher capacity is developed.

A facilitator and leader in education, her peers commend her ability to develop relationships, increase student achievement, develop a positive culture in the schools, develop purposeful strategies, and lead with intentionality.

Sonya is a member of Delta Sigma Theta Sorority, Inc., National Council of Teachers of Mathematics, and Gamma Beta Phi Honor Society.

She has a bachelor of science degree in education, a master of education degree in reading, and an education specialists degree in administration from Middle Tennessee State University. She also has an education specialists degree in educational leadership, and an education doctorate degree in educational leadership from Carson Newman University.

To connect, email her at swj019@gmail.com

Courtney Taylor is the bestselling co-author of *Soulful Prayers* and *The Gift That Keeps On Giving*. She is an advocate for nontoxic, godly relationships, and is also the CEO and founder of Courtney's Closet Outreach, Inc., a Texas-based 501(c)(3) non-profit organization dedicated to donating essential items to those in need.

A licensed evangelist and businesswoman extraordinaire, Courtney is a catalyst for intentional living and encourages people to seek God, the Creator, to reveal their purpose.

Courtney's proudest moment is the God-given idea to host her very first B.A.T. Men Conference, an event tailored to empower young males by providing essential information pertaining to their personal growth and development.

Courtney prays to make an impact in the world through community outreach and by spreading the gospel and love of Jesus Christ. She unapologetically loves God with all of her heart. She deeply loves her family, friends, and everyone.

To connect, email her at ctayenterprises@gmail.com

Rev. Dr. Janie Dowdy-Dandridge, D Min. has been called to impact the kingdom of God as a global visionary voice. She moves grief and loss into action using her narrative leadership style of ministry and transforms pain into purpose. As an author, preacher, pastor, catalyst for change, professional clinical chaplain, life coach, motivational speaker, entrepreneur, advocate, and activist, she is a force for change. Dr. Janie Dowdy-Dandridge creates a high-energy and spirited attitude to empower others to move forward from the lessons she learned about grief and loss. She is godly proud of her new book, *You Have What It Takes to Lead: What's Stopping You?*

Dr. Dowdy-Dandridge has established a 501(c)(3) non-profit organization where she serves as the executive director of Tennessee Game Changers United for Justice and Equality, a grassroots organization that advocates for individuals who suffer from trauma and loss.

Learn more at www.facebook.com/janie.dowdydandridge

Reverend Lillie I. Sanders is a retired educator and an ordained associate minister at Watts Chapel Missionary Baptist Church in Raleigh, North Carolina. Lillie's servanthood at Watts Chapel MBC includes being a student, creative teacher, and gifted preacher of God's Word. She is a Bible curriculum writer and Bible workshop presenter.

Reverend Lillie received her B.S. in social science and M.A. in library science from North Carolina Central University in Durham, North Carolina, and an endorsement in elementary school administration from George Mason University in Fairfax, Virginia.

She received her masters of biblical studies degree and her masters of divinity degree from Maple Springs Baptist Bible College and Seminary in Capitol Heights, Maryland. She received a certificate in Christian education from Virginia Union University, in Richmond, Virginia. Reverend Lillie also studied at John Wesley Theological Seminary in Washington, D.C. and attended Preachers' Seminar Training at Gordon-Conwell Theological Seminary in Hamilton, Massachusetts.

To connect, email her at hegotupon3@nc.rr.com

Rev. Dr. Sonja V. Brown Deloatch, a woman of great faith and fortitude, has been referred as "The Singer Preacher." Sonja currently works as a licensed social worker, providing services to Veterans who suffer with mental illness. Sonja is also the senior pastor of Winters Chapel African Methodist Episcopal Church (AME) in Lebanon, Tennessee, and an endorsed chaplain. She completed her undergraduate degree in psychology, and received a master's degree of divinity at Shaw University as well as a master's degree in social work from Fayetteville State University. Her proudest academic accomplishment was being confirmed as the First Woman of the 13th. Episcopal District of the AME Church with a doctorate in theology from the historical Payne Theological Seminary.

Sonja is a member of Delta Sigma Theta Sorority, Inc., Order of Eastern Star, the Association of Clinical Pastoral Education, and the National Black Chaplains Association.

Sonja has two adult children and two grandchildren.

To connect, email her at jamaso0203@gmail.com

Clara Matimba was born and raised in Harare, Zimbabwe. She is a mother of three daughters and one son-in-law. She received a bachelor's degree in business studies from Dallas Baptist University, is a licensed vocational nurse, and has obtained several Microsoft IT certifications. For the last nineteen and a half years, she has been working in the telecommunications industry. And for the last six years, she has been working PRN as a nurse.

In her spare time, she volunteers for The Salvation Army feeding the homeless and mentoring elementary-aged girls in the Lewisville School District. Her passion is to see others excel no matter their circumstances, and she advocates for healthy living and exercise. Clara is an avid traveler who enjoys life to the fullest, knowing that her accomplishments would not be possible without God.

To connect, email her at claramatimba@gmail.com

Jahara Davis was born in Darmstadt, Germany, and raised in Fayetteville, North Carolina. She received her undergraduate degree from North Carolina Central University, majoring in English Literature. In 2014, she began teaching English at E.E. Smith High School in Fayetteville, North Carolina.

In 2017, Jahara relocated to Charlotte, North Carolina, and joined the staff of West Charlotte High School. During her first year, she was nominated West Charlotte High Teacher of the Year. Months after, Jahara was named Project L.I.F.T. Learning Community Teacher of the Year. Within the same year, she accepted an award during CIAA Education Day for Food Lion's 2018 Outstanding High School Educator Award.

Jahara was an editor for *The Prevailing Woman* magazine, appeared on Fox 46's *Charlotte Good Day*, and was a guest speaker on 101.9 in Charlotte, North Carolina. Jahara currently works at Wilson STEM Academy as an 8th. grade English Language Arts teacher.

Jahara has two beautiful children, Carter and Davis.

To connect, email her at jaharadavis88@gmail.com

Leroy Francis Jr., a native Texan, was born in Houston and raised in Dallas. He earned a bachelor's in business management and is a proud member of his beloved fraternity Omega Psi Phi. After spending 24 years with Coca-Cola Enterprises, Leroy moved to the logistical side of transportation with AutoZone Distribution.

Leroy is a loving husband, father, and grandfather who operates in the gift of service. Due to his desire to keep young males on the straight and narrow, he has served with the Omega Psi Phi Fraternity Sparks Mentoring Program and uses his story to mentor and guide young boys to become powerful men. He also hopes to continue operating the family business—Community Funeral Home of Tyler, Texas—alongside his father and family.

To connect, email him at 19gravedigger11@gmail.com

Sherry Wurgler is a mother of four grown children and a grandmother to five. They are her joy, her passion, and her motivation to always be the best version of herself. Sherry is also a practicing RN working in the field of psychiatry.

She is a bestselling author and has written in several anthologies. Her memoir, *Surviving Ritual Abuse*, ranked as a number one bestseller on Amazon.

Sherry is working towards becoming an online coach and will be helping others regain the power of their voice to make choices to live life to the fullest!

To connect, email her at wurgler3@msn.com

Charmaine Roots Castillo is a writer who discovered her passion for writing at the age of 63 after publishing her first book, *Who Killed My Son? A Mother's Wait for Justice.* Writing about the events that surrounded her son's murder opened her heart to share her unshakeable faith in God through her second book, *Who Killed My Son? Contending for Peace.*

Charmaine collaborated with nationally acclaimed author Cheryl Polote-Williamson in the bestselling book, *Soulful Prayers: The Power of Intentional Communication with God*, and shared her heartfelt, intentional prayer concerning her wait for justice.

She founded The LaFondé Experience, LLC, which is a platform to release her God-given gifts to inspire the brokenhearted and deliver the message that "You are never too old to pursue your dreams."

Charmaine is an avid tennis player and bowler born in Richmond, Virginia, and now resides in Tampa, Florida, with her husband Amos.

Learn more at www.56silverfoxx.com

Heidi Lewis-Ivey is a multi-bestselling and national award-winning author, sought-after speaker, motivator, and teacher who influences international audiences with her authenticity and bold style of delivery. Having experienced the pain and stigma of domestic violence, she was able to discover her voice through her writing. She holds an MBA with a concentration in organizational leadership and is a member of Delta Mu Delta International Honor Society for Business. Recognized as a savvy leader and for her ability to train and mentor leaders, she serves as the executive director of PureSpring Institute.

Heidi is host of the *In My Father's House* radio broadcast where she inspires audiences to live free, live holistically, and live out loud! She also hosts the Can I Rest Awhile gathering.

Heidi currently resides in Boston, Massachusetts, and her mother is her greatest inspiration.

Learn more at www.booklaunch.io/heidi/author-heidi

Larry C. Brown is an eastern North Carolina native who currently resides in Raleigh, North Carolina. At an early age, he gave his life to Christ and strives to live Christ-filled. A cancer survivor of two years, Larry enjoys singing and is a member of the prestigious 100 Men in Black choir based in Durham, North Carolina. He also sings with the male gospel chorus at First Baptist Church of Roxboro, North Carolina. While he has worked in the auto parts industry for over 20 years, his hobbies include working on cars and writing both love and spiritual poems. Larry has co-authored one book, the Amazon bestseller, *Soulful Prayers: The Power of Intentional Communication with God*. He is a gym enthusiast and most early mornings that is where he can be found.

Larry believes that all things are possible as long as you have Jesus Christ in your life.

To connect, email him at LarryCBrown063@gmail.com

Sharla Thomas is the founder and CEO of the 501(c)(3), My Rare Son Isaiah PH Warrior Foundation, Inc. The foundation's mission is to inspire, educate, and leverage resources to support pulmonary hypertension research programs, with initiatives that focus on improving the lives of those suffering from pulmonary hypertension.

Sharla has a servant's heart and a passion to serve others. She is active in several community organizations in Dallas, Texas. She is also the wife of Anthony Thomas, and mother to Isaiah and Anthony Thomas Jr.

Sharla gives thanks to God and her family and friends whom have supported her.

To connect, email her at myraresonisaiah@gmail.com

Keith L. Maddox is the embodiment of anointed preaching, teaching, and prayer, from the early blessing of salvation at 14 years old, to holding Bible studies during lunch periods at school, to a journey through Christian education and ordaining, to pastoring and being an in-demand speaker.

Louisiana-born and California-raised, Maddox was installed in 2004 as pastor of Palm Springs Apostolic Church, which later became Grace Apostolic Church Inc., where he and his wife pastored for twelve years. Elder Maddox has served as an instructor at Aenon School of Theology; chaplain; and a licensed, ordained elder of the Pentecostal Assemblies of the World (PAW). He is a consistently sought-out speaker, evangelist, and teacher for conferences, revivals, and seminars.

Elder Keith Maddox is the husband of one wife, Lady Dretona Maddox. They are the proud parents of six children. They are also grandparents of three.

Learn more at www.KeithLMaddox.com

Camille McKenzie has been teaching and preaching the Word of God since she was in high school. God's Word has been the inspiration of her life, throughout her life. Now it is Camille's mission to give back what God has given to her by inspiring women to be transformed by God's Word!

Camille's company, Camille Inspires, is focused on teaching Christian women how to understand and apply God's Word in taking care of their bodies, emotions, and spirit. Camille is a firm believer that there is no problem that God and His Word cannot solve, and she inspires women to believe the same.

Camille's brand is a reflection of who she is: focused, disciplined, committed, and loving. As a certified lifestyle coach, she uses the powerful combination of coaching techniques with the Word of God to guide women to the One who transforms lives!

Learn more at www.CamilleInspires.com

Ernetta Caldwell is an actress, inspirational speaker, and registered nurse. Ernetta is the founder and CEO of Beauty For Ashes Transformations, LLC, where she inspires woman that have gone through a separation or divorce to overcome by implementing self-love, healing, and restoration. She provides private life coaching, workshops, and speaking engagements. She is a bestselling co-author in *Soulful Prayers* and completed her solo book project *A Journey To a Healed Heart; Healing Through a Painful Divorce*.

Ernetta is a founding board member of the non-profit, A Giving Heart Project, to help serve the less fortunate in her community. She has been on tour with the 2017 Gospel Image award-winning stage play, *Bad Manners at The Dinner Table*, with Cast Me Not full services agency. Ernetta and her husband, Anthony, reside in South Carolina. They have three beautiful children and four grandchildren.

Ernetta's goals are to passionately help others in need and to complete her God-given assignments while on this earth.

Learn more at www.ErnettaCaldwell.com

Scott Wilson has been a professional business management consultant since 1998, achieving success as a team member creating an over $400 million per year outsourcing business at PwC Consulting, and as a member of the deal team during IBM's PwC Consulting acquisition. During his time in management consulting, he closed over $2 billion dollars worth of transactions in the outsourcing and digital transformation space.

However, Scott's greatest success was his personal journey to becoming a recovered alcoholic. His journey led him to learn that he was not God, showed him who God is, and allowed him to find his purpose and passion in life. Scott is the proud father of two daughters, Mackenzie and Caroline, and his son, Grayson. He is actively involved in local recovery groups, and volunteers with the Coppell Police Department and his church. Scott is also the co-founder of Gratitude and Grace Consulting, with his business partner and good friend, Todd Storch.

Learn more at www.gratitudeandgraceconsulting.com

Reverend Trinette Barrie is a called, anointed, and appointed Christian wife and mother whose mission is to help people live better lives spiritually, emotionally, academically, and mentally. She grew up in the Los Angeles area and was called to preach in 2004. Subsequently, she heeded the call and was licensed to preach in 2011.

Trinette is an inspiring counselor, professor, and scholar who holds four degrees: B.A. Theater Arts, MEd College Student Affairs, MS Counseling Psychology (MFT), and M.A. Counseling Ministry. She has served in higher education for over 20 years and holds certifications to teach, interpret, and counsel in the MBTI, Strong, CliftonStrengths, and Prepare/Enrich.

Trinette is a dynamic speaker, gifted minister, and teacher. She is witty, entertaining, and engaging to audiences of all ages. She loves to inspire, motivate, educate, and empower her listeners to learn something new about God, themselves, and their true purpose and journey in life.

Learn more at www.TrinetteBarrie.com

Kim Coles has delighted audiences all over the world for over 35 years. As a beloved and multifaceted actress and comedian, she has appeared on groundbreaking TV shows such as *In Living Color* and *Living Single*. A sought-after online academy teacher and intuitive story coach, Kim also guides women on the incredible healing journey of story-telling and leveraging their own authentic stories to inspire others to learn, laugh, and leave their own powerful legacy. She is the author of four bestselling books, and she is an engaging and life changing keynote speaker.

Learn more at www.kimcoles.tv

Cheryl Polote-Williamson is a global media executive whose purpose is to help people share their stories and attain healing. She is the visionary behind thirteen bestselling books, including *Words from the Spirit for the Spirit*, *Affirmed*, and the Soul Talk series. She holds a bachelor of science in criminal justice and is also a certified life coach and the executive director of the 501(c)(3), Soul Reborn.

Cheryl has amassed numerous accolades such as featured author at the NAACP and Congressional Black Caucus Conference, 2017 winner of the IALA Literary Trailblazer of the Year award, and executive producer of the year for the stage play *Soul Purpose*. In addition, Cheryl's first film production was selected for the Greater Cleveland Urban Film Festival and the BronzeLens Film Festival. Her upcoming projects include *Soulful Prayers, Vol. 2*, and the films *Saving Clarissa* and *Illegal Rose*.

Cheryl resides in Texas with her husband, Russell Williamson Sr. They have three children and two grandchildren.

Learn more at www.cherylpwilliamson.com

purposely created
PUBLISHING

CREATING DISTINCTIVE BOOKS
WITH INTENTIONAL RESULTS

We're a collaborative group of creative masterminds
with a mission to produce high-quality books to position
you for monumental success in the marketplace.

Our professional team of writers, editors, designers,
and marketing strategists work closely together to ensure
that every detail of your book is a clear representation
of the message in your writing.

Want to know more?
Write to us at info@publishyourgift.com
or call (888) 949-6228

Discover great books, exclusive offers, and more at
www.PublishYourGift.com

Connect with us on social media

@publishyourgift

CPSIA information can be obtained
at www.ICGtesting.com
Printed in the USA
FSHW021509240420
69487FS